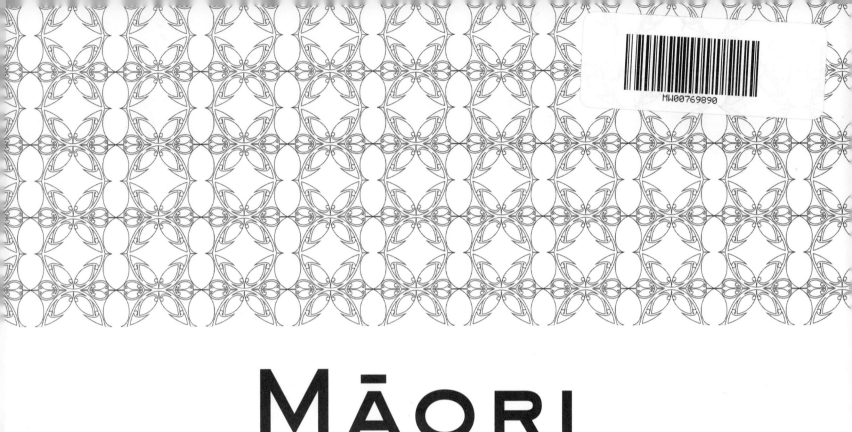

MĀORI
PATTERNS

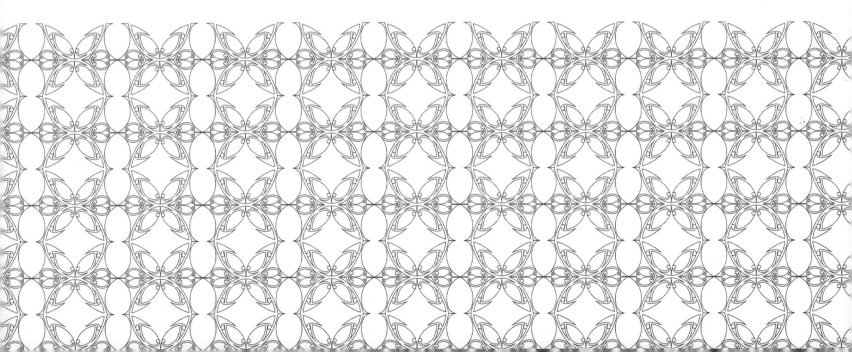

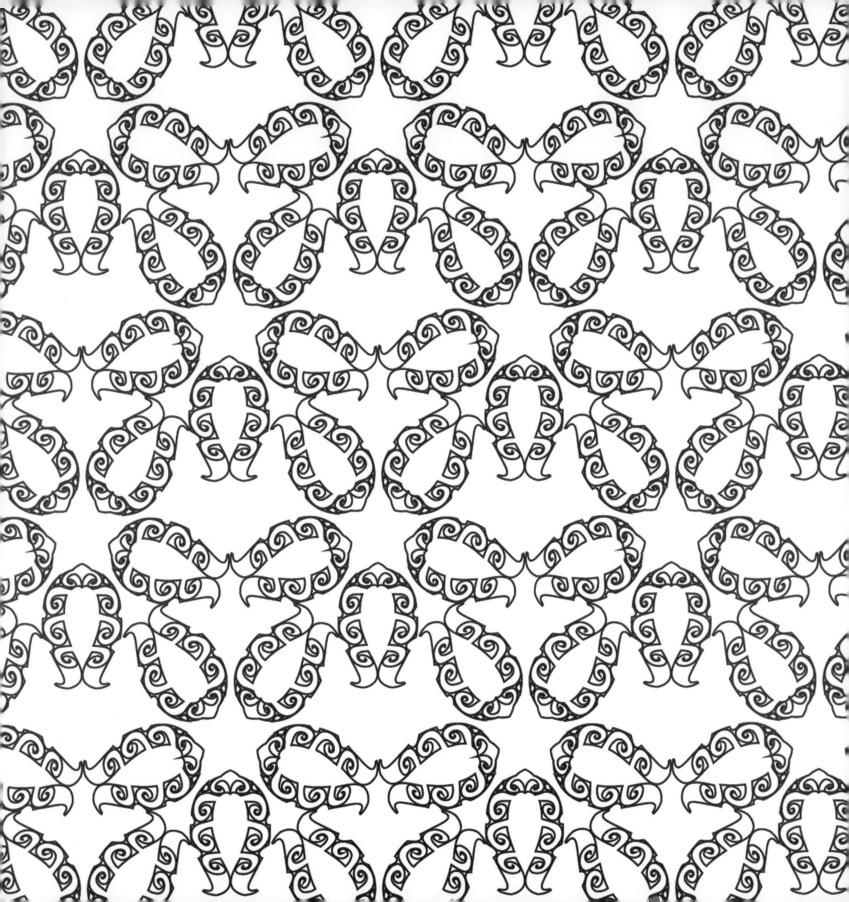

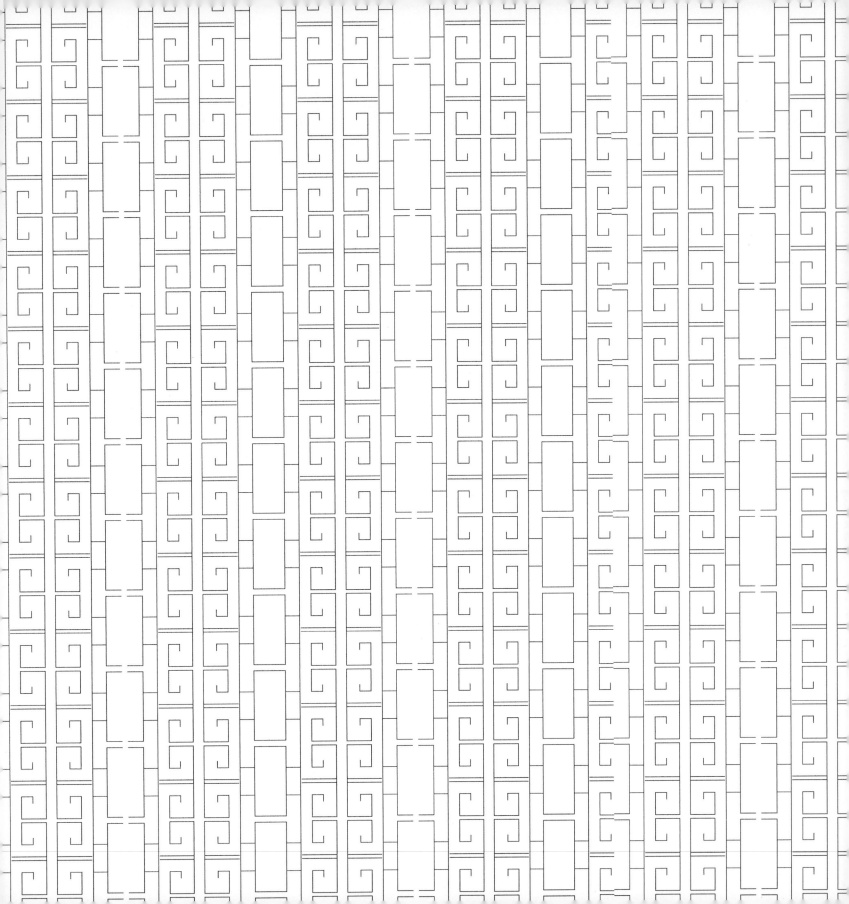

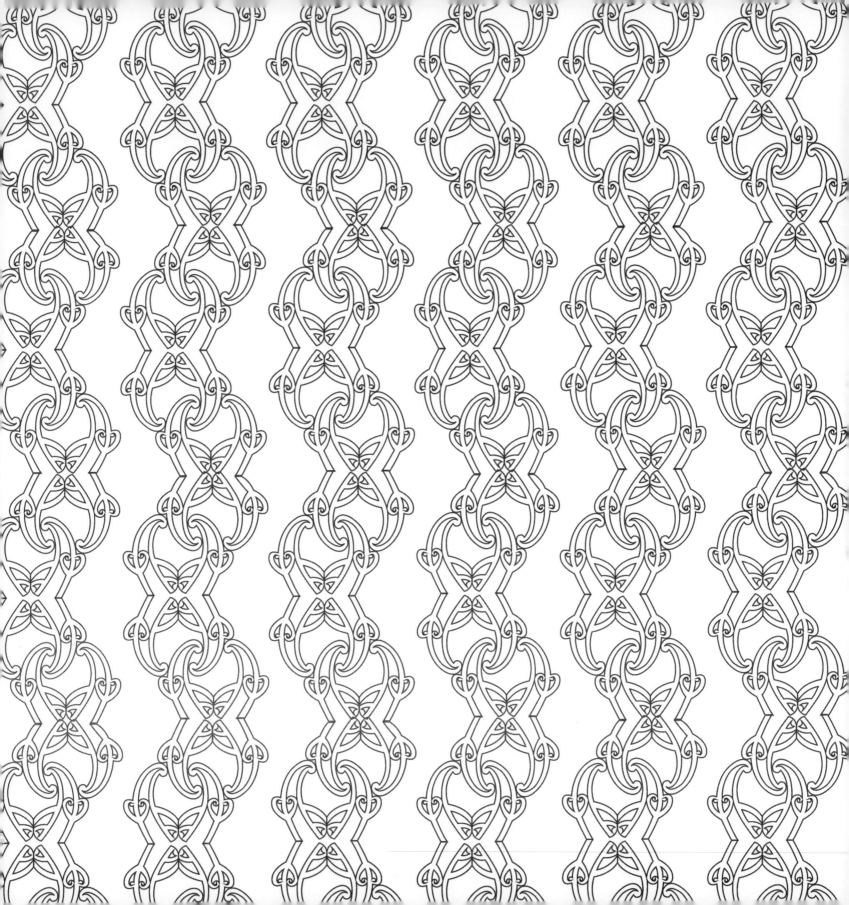

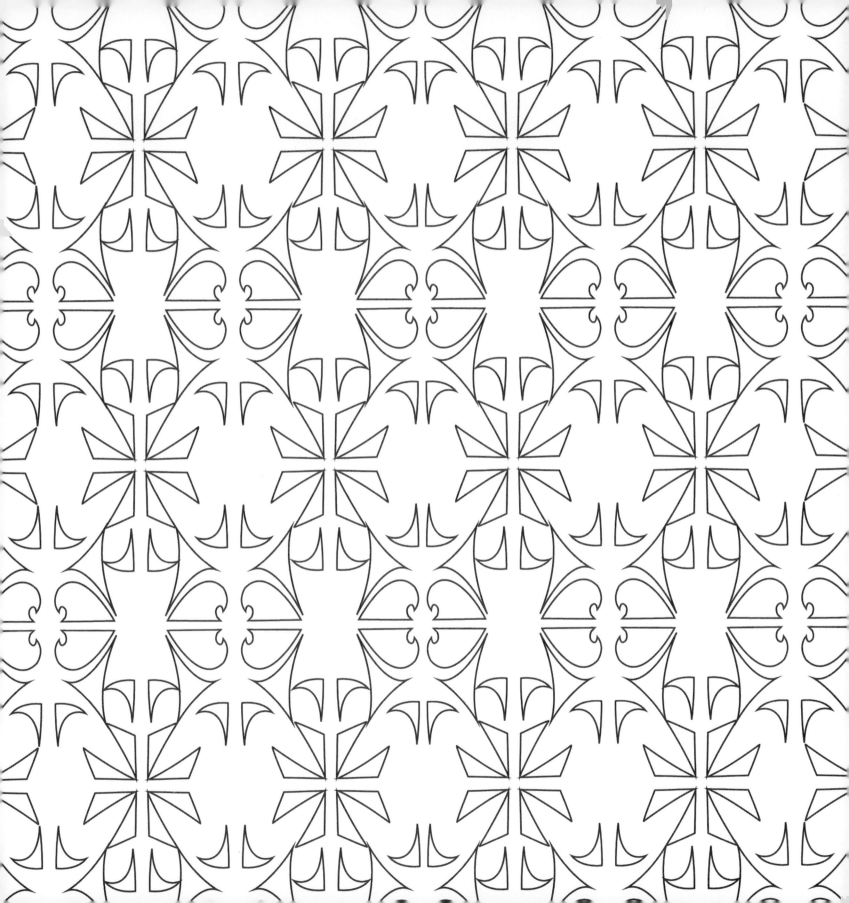

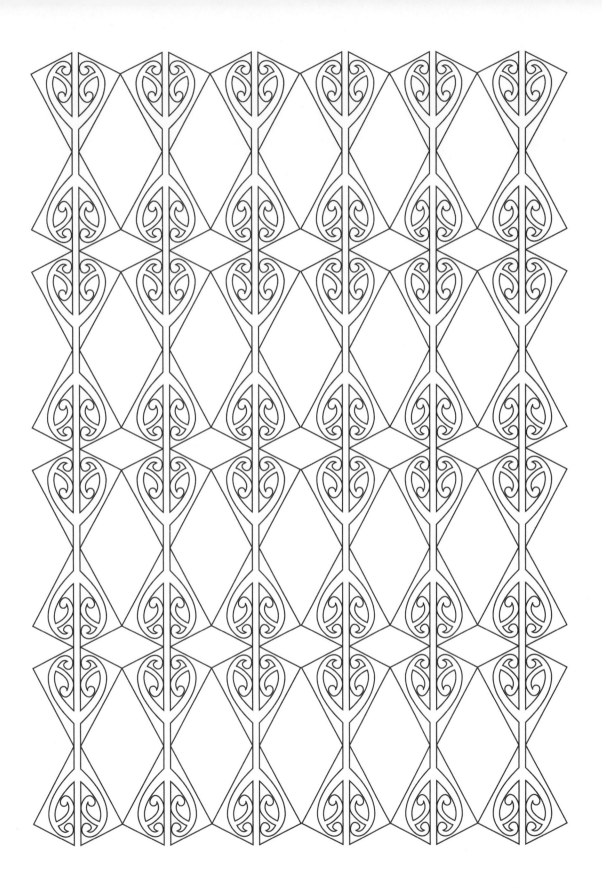

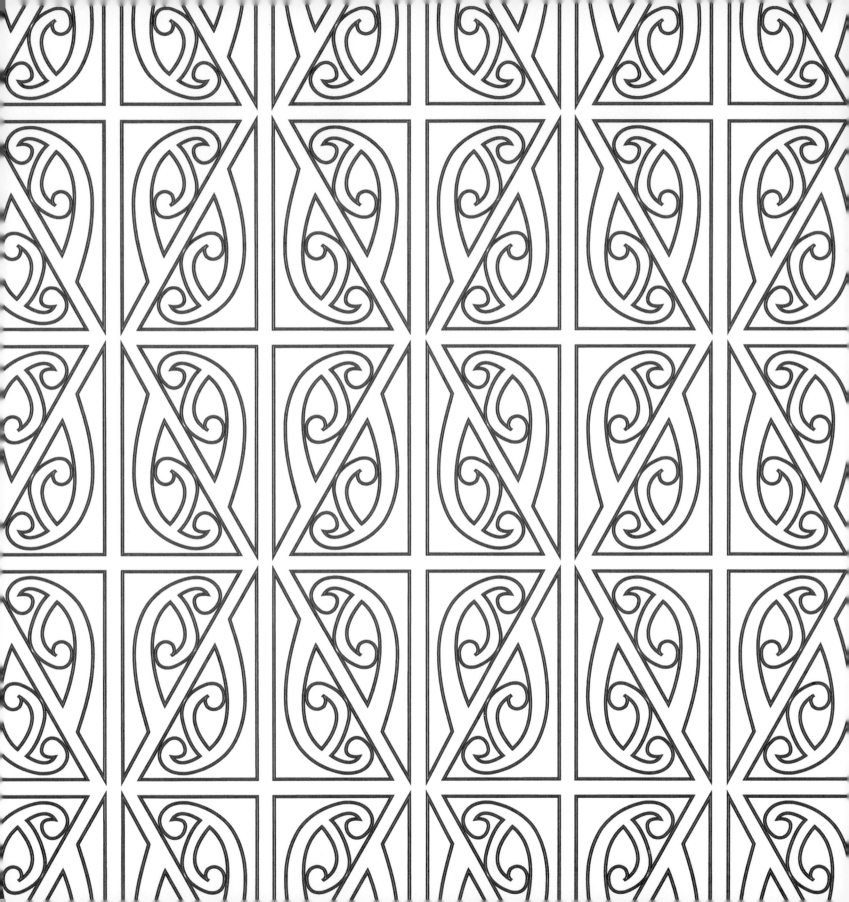

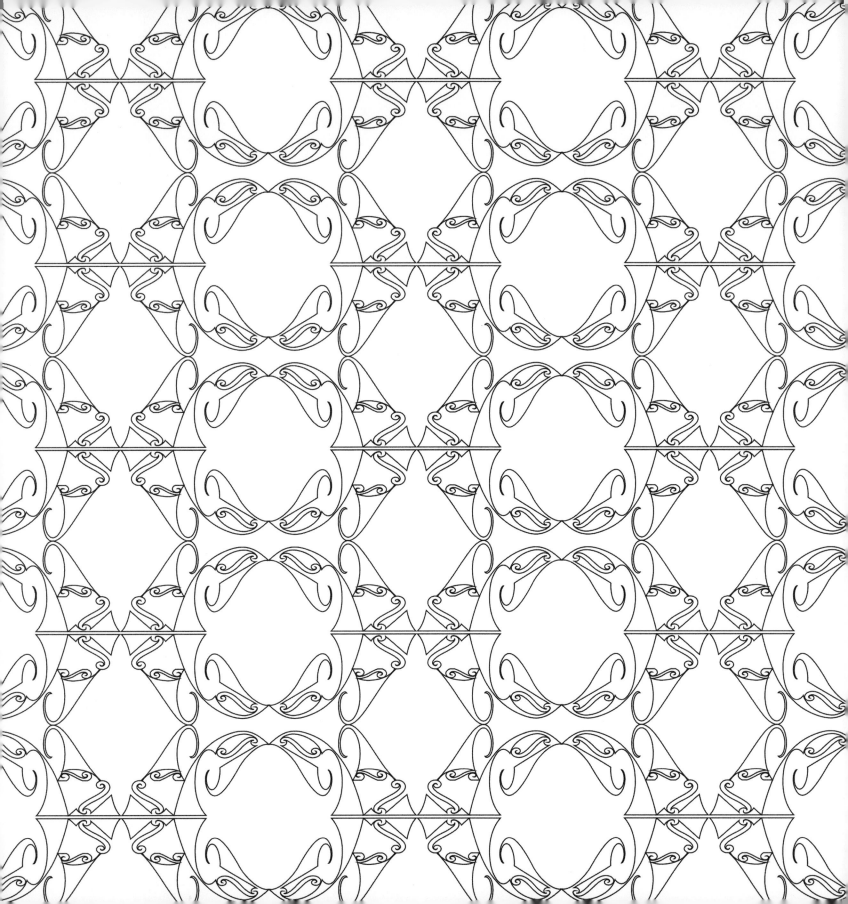

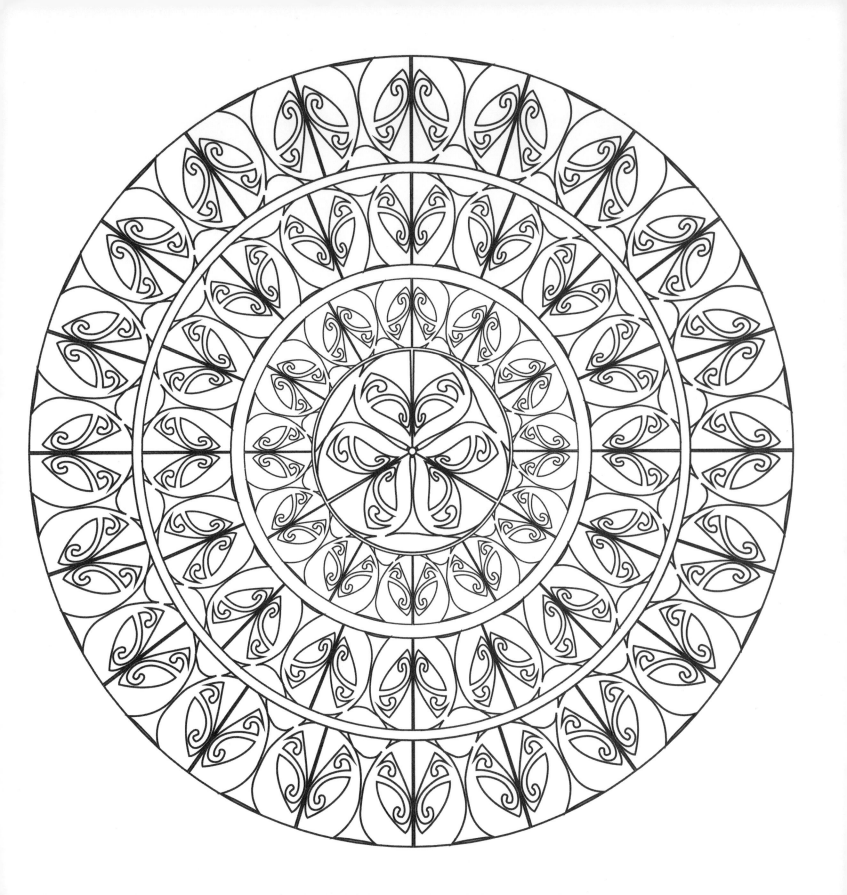

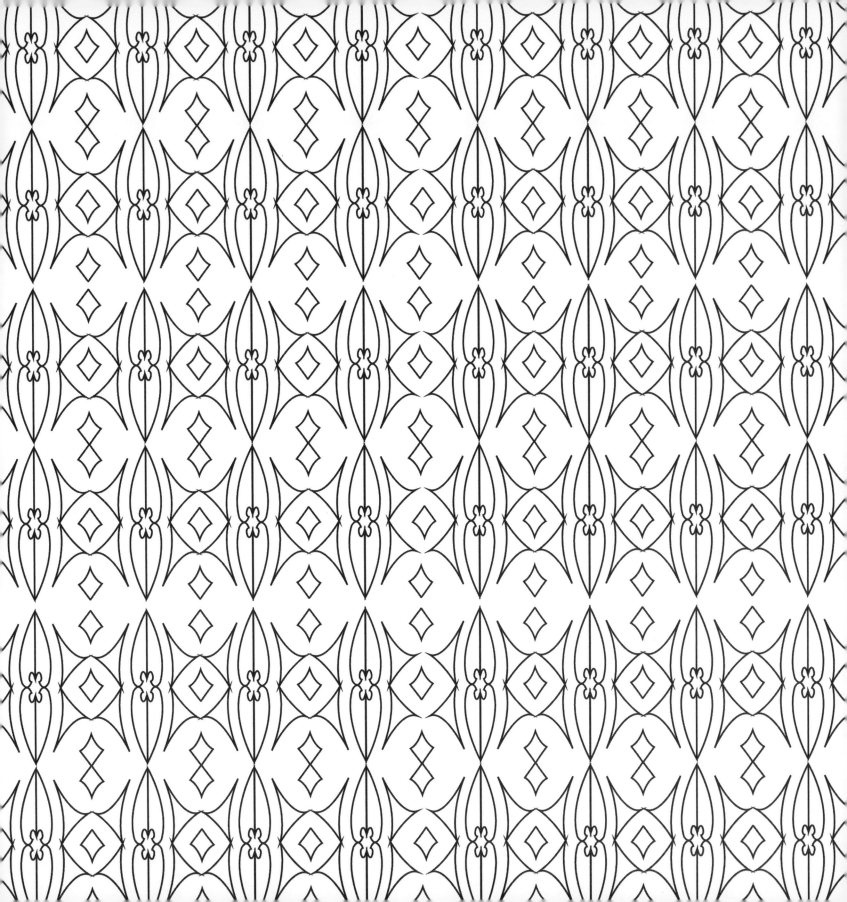

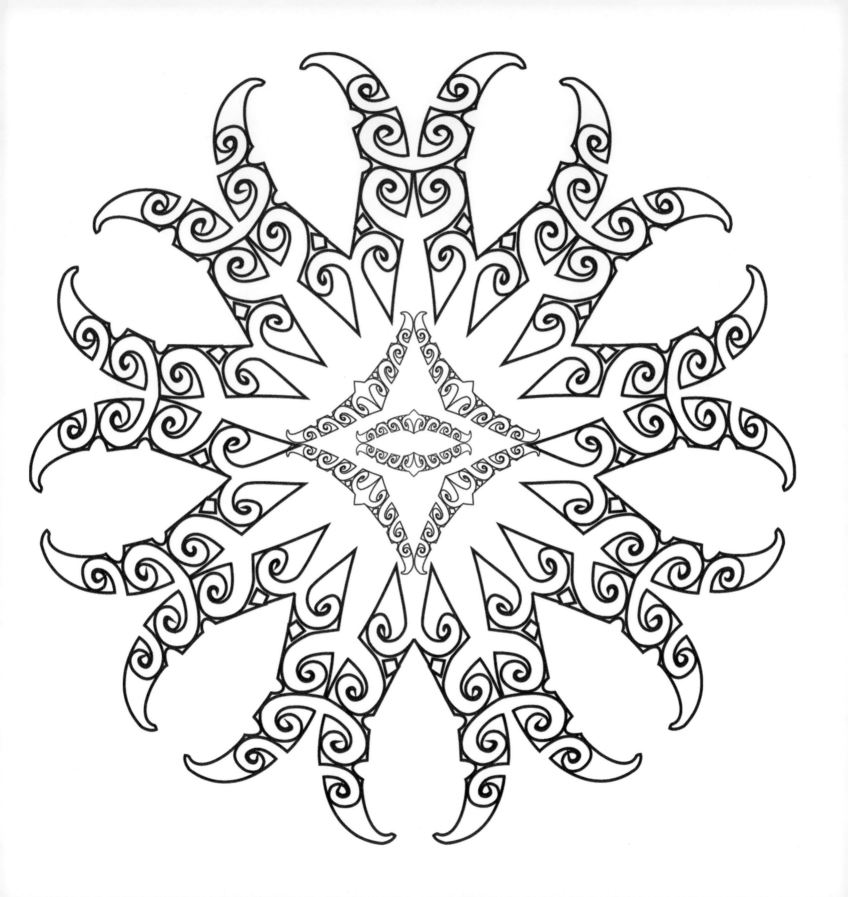

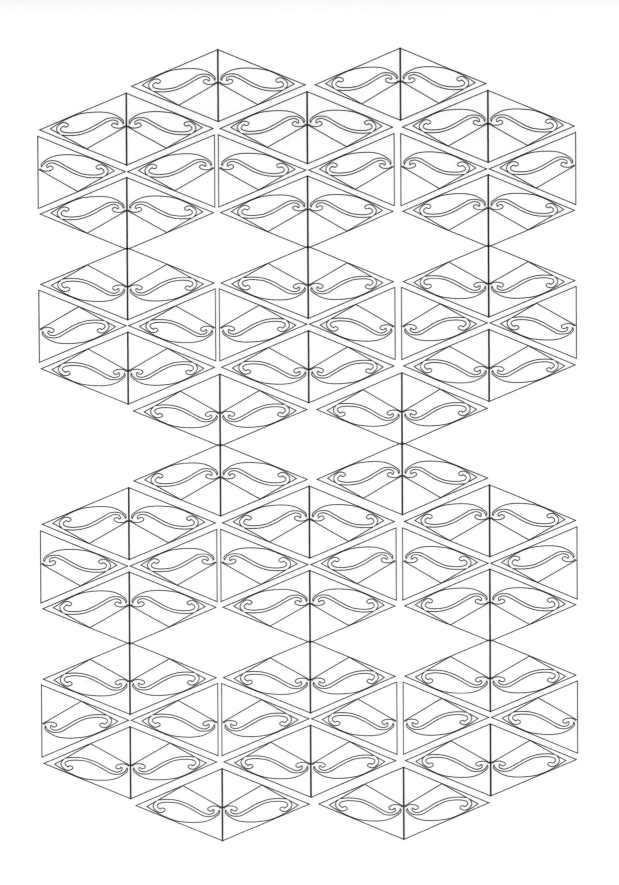

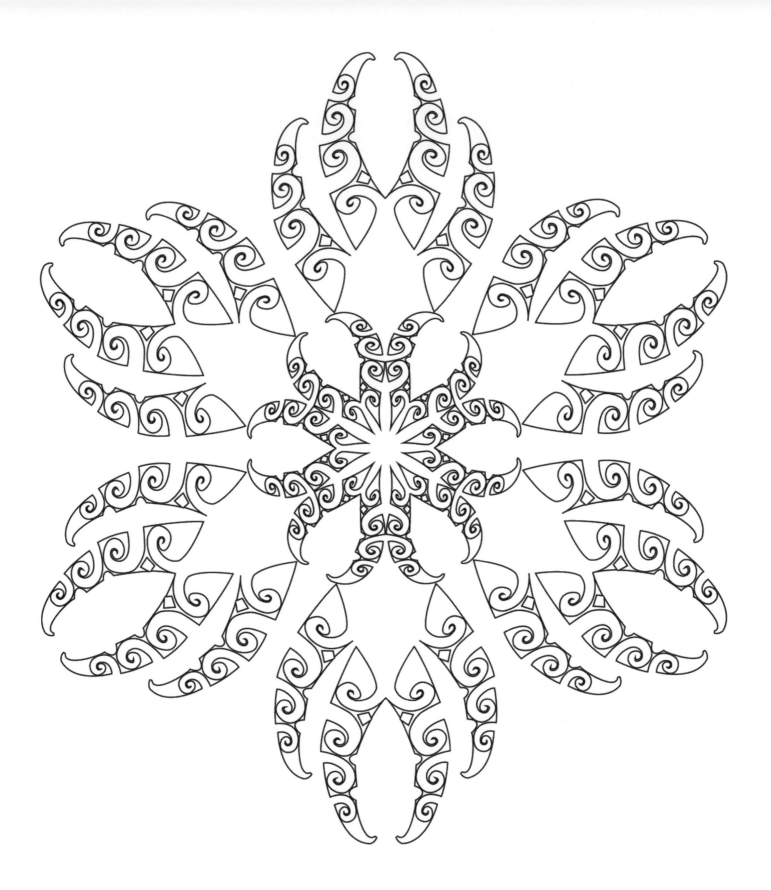

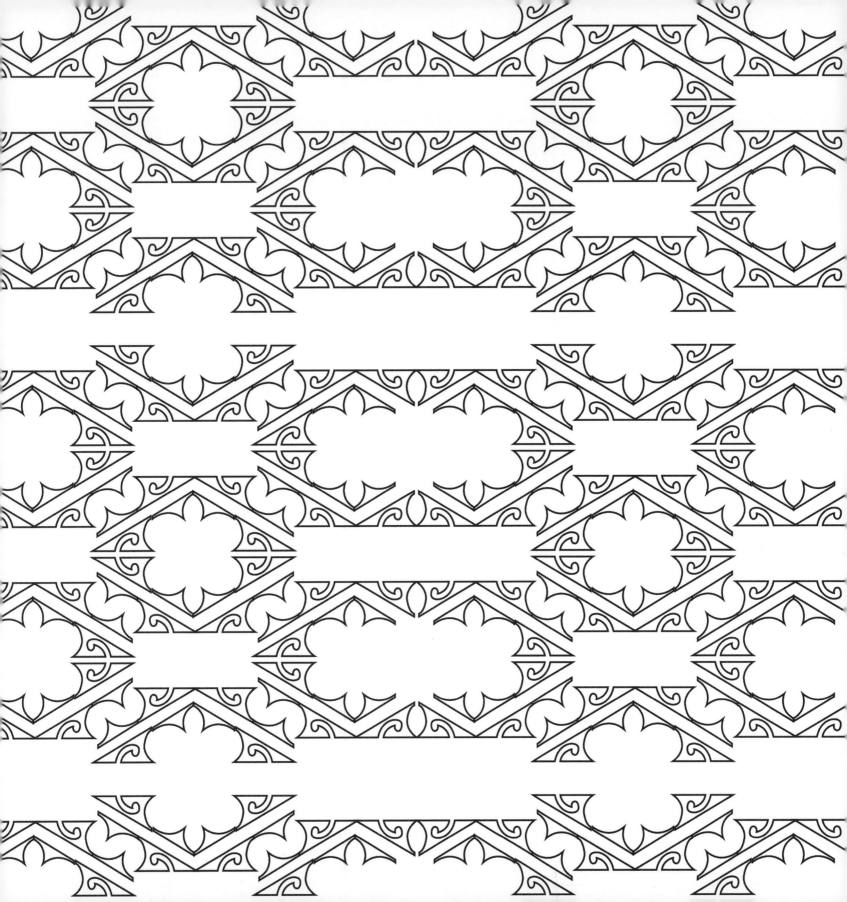

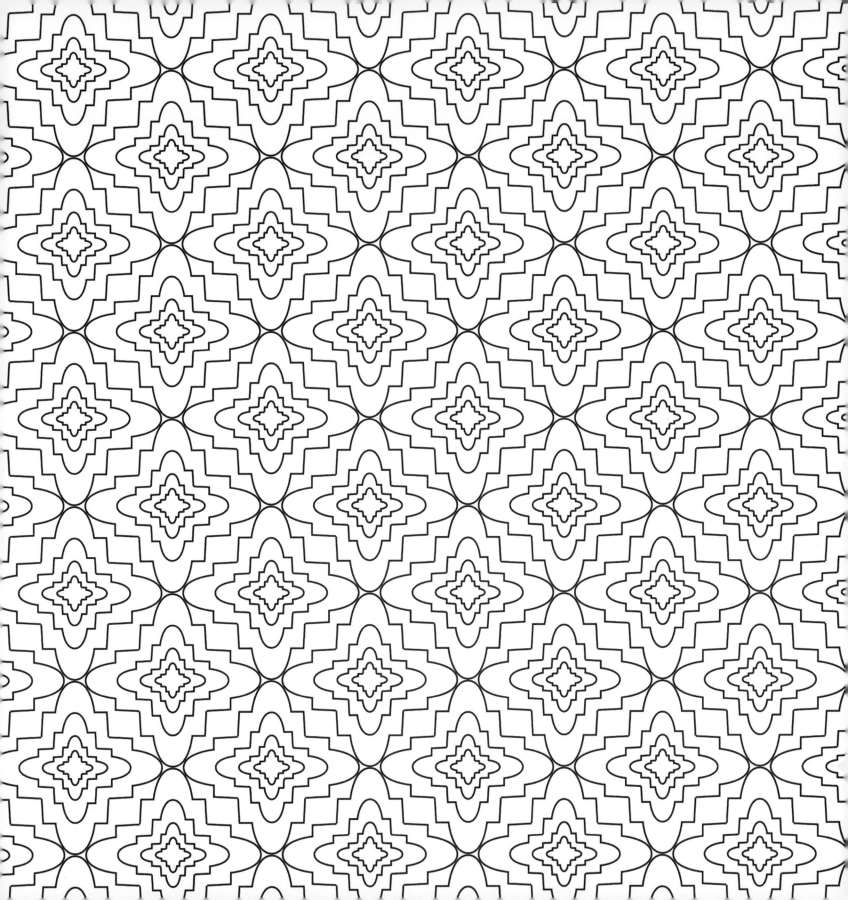

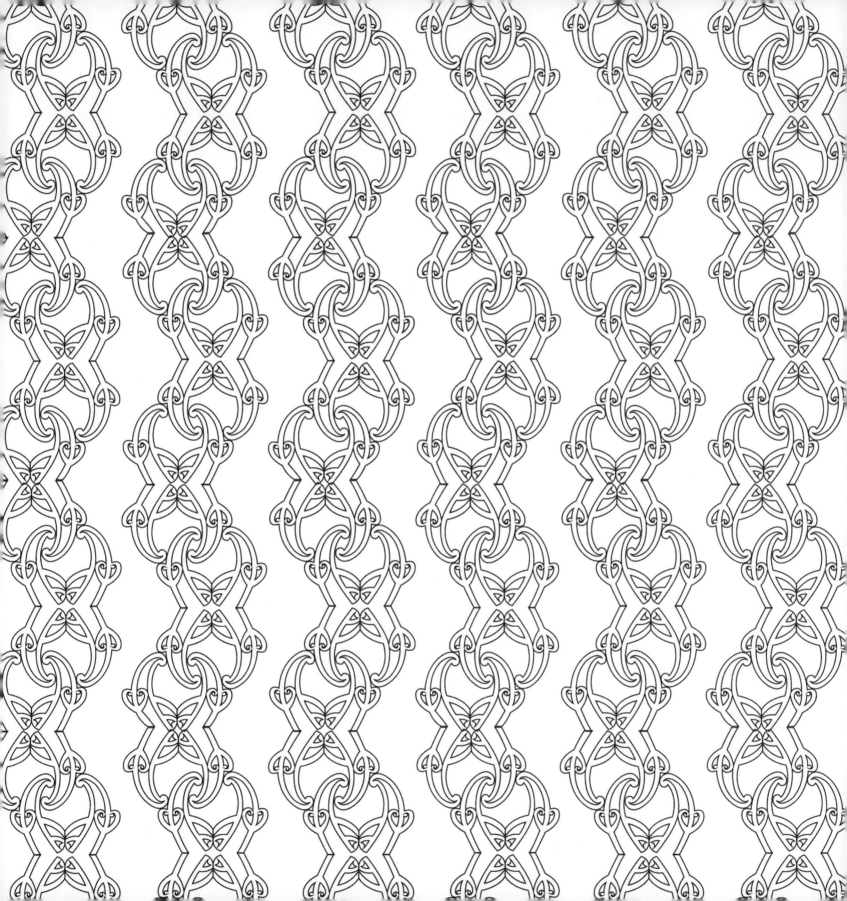

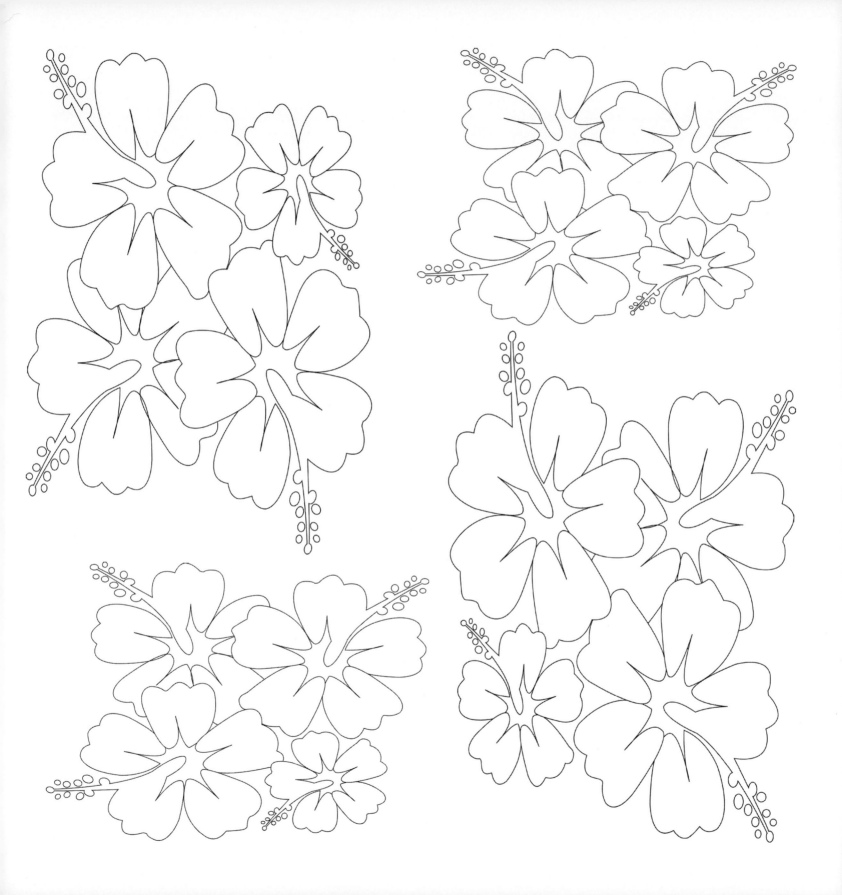

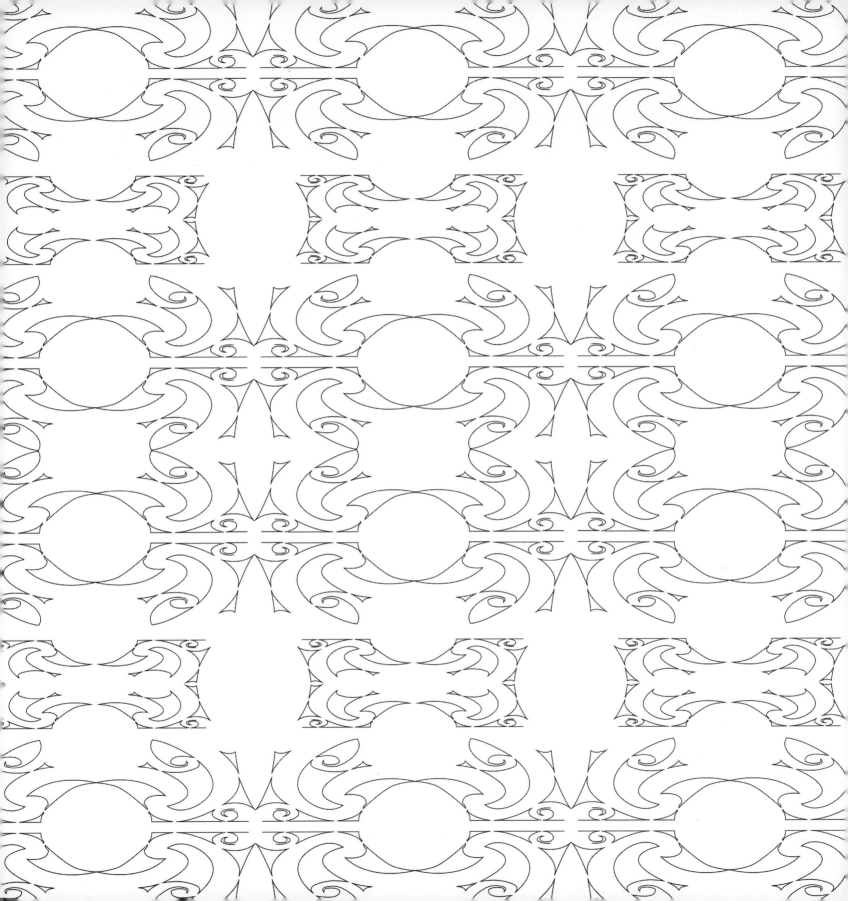

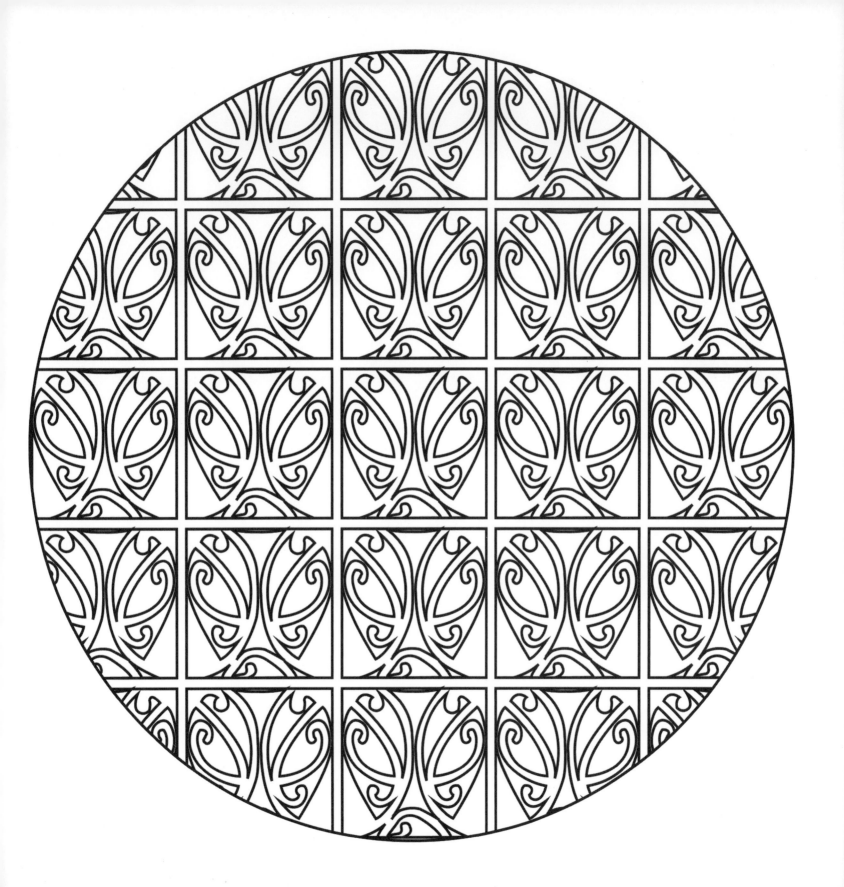

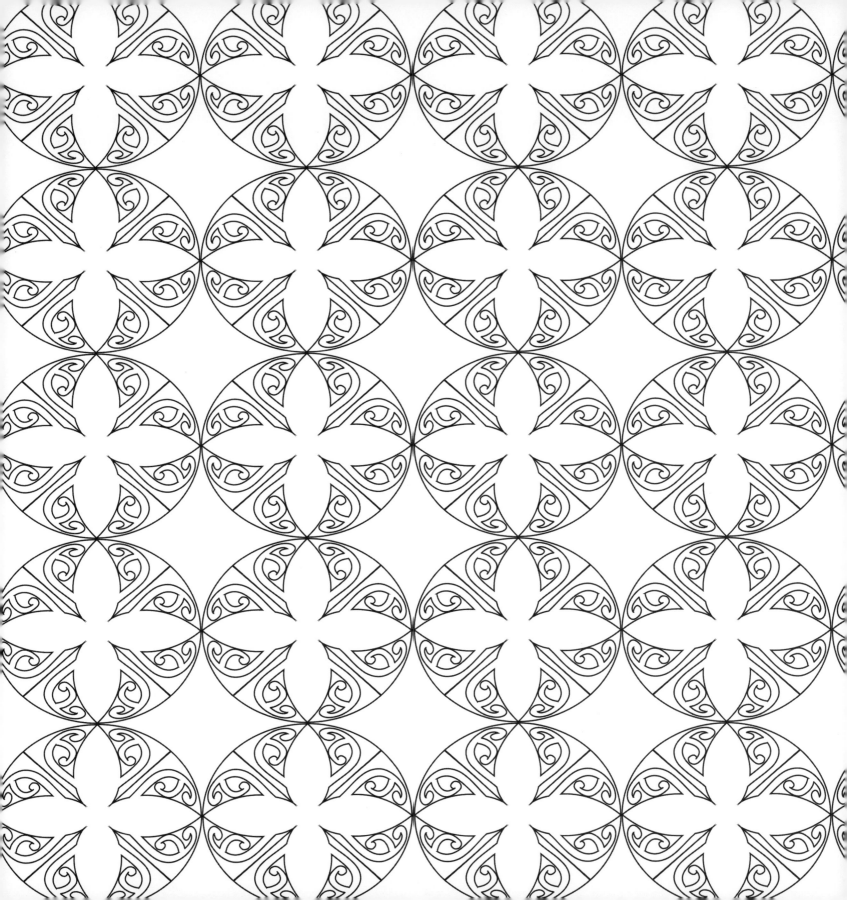

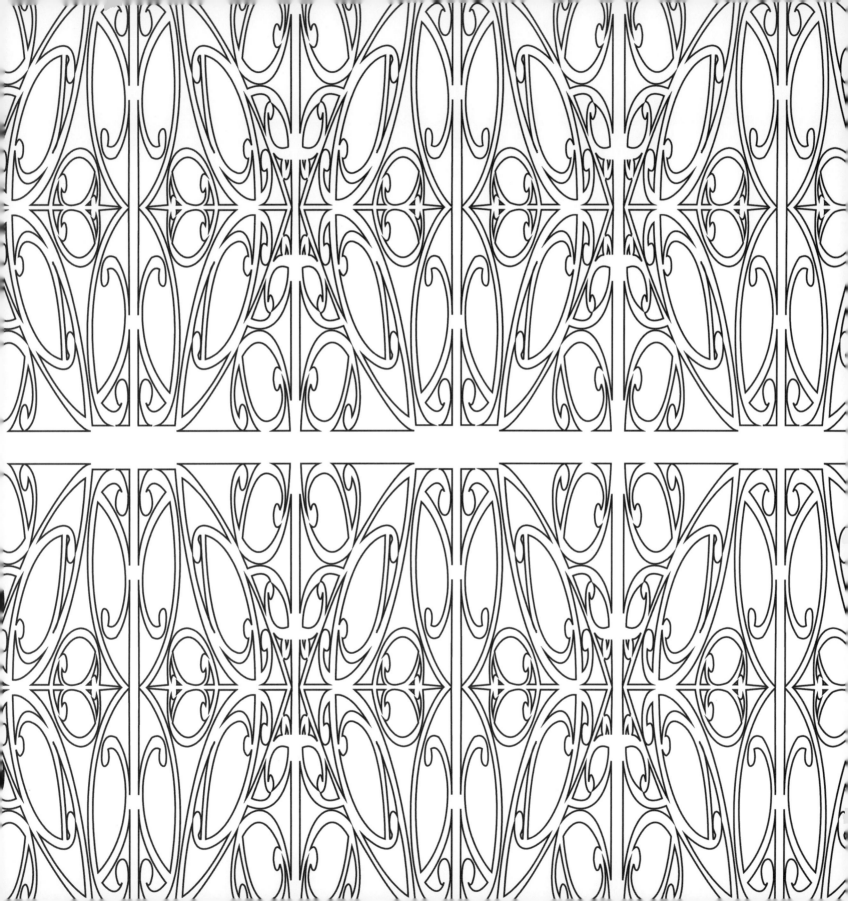

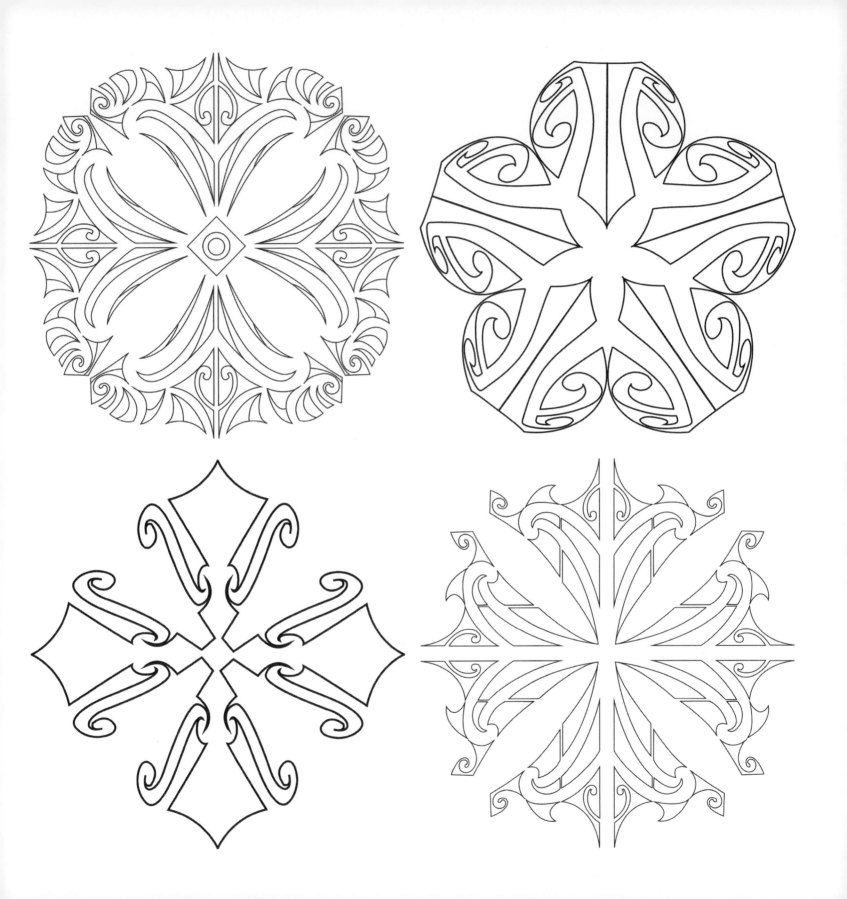

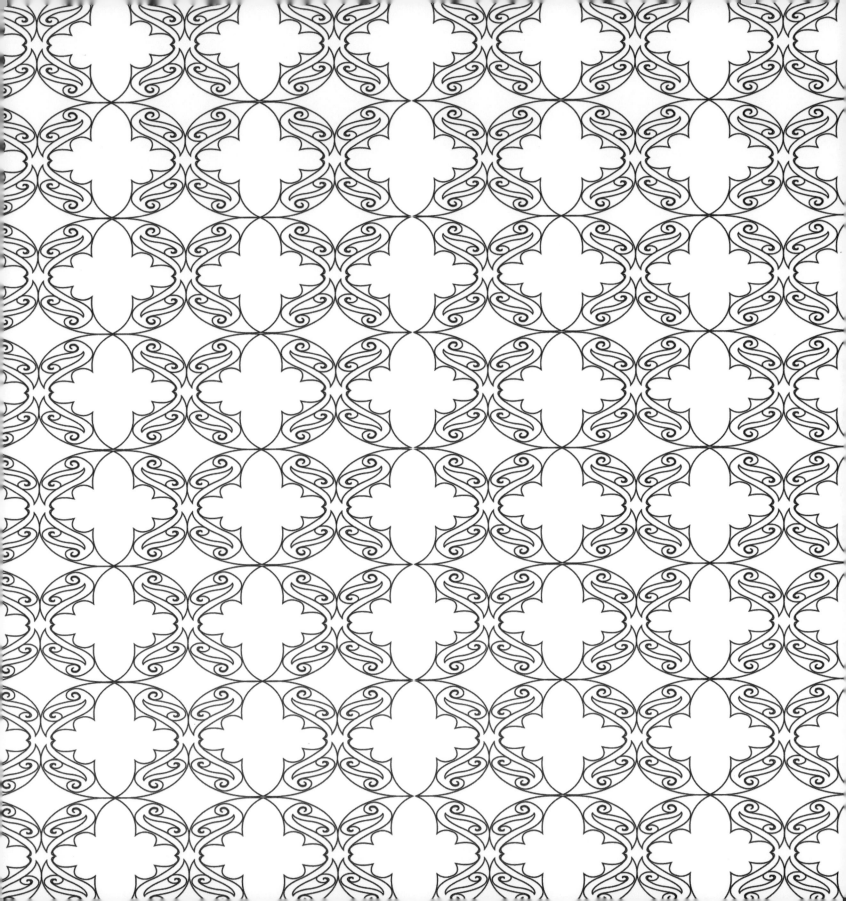

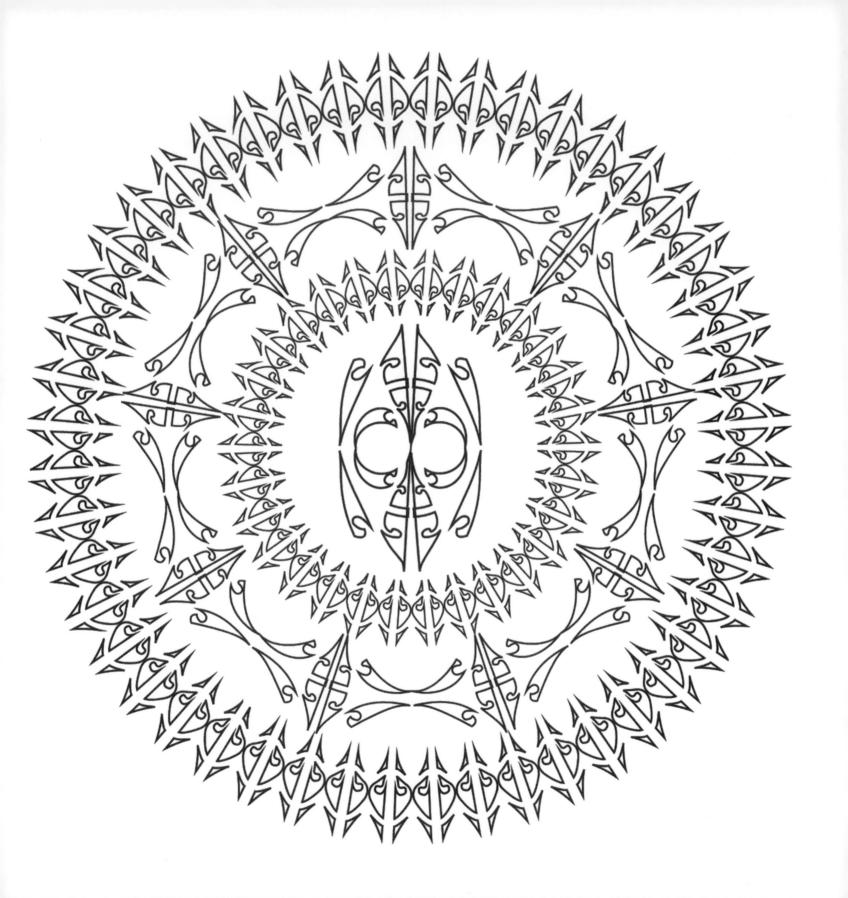

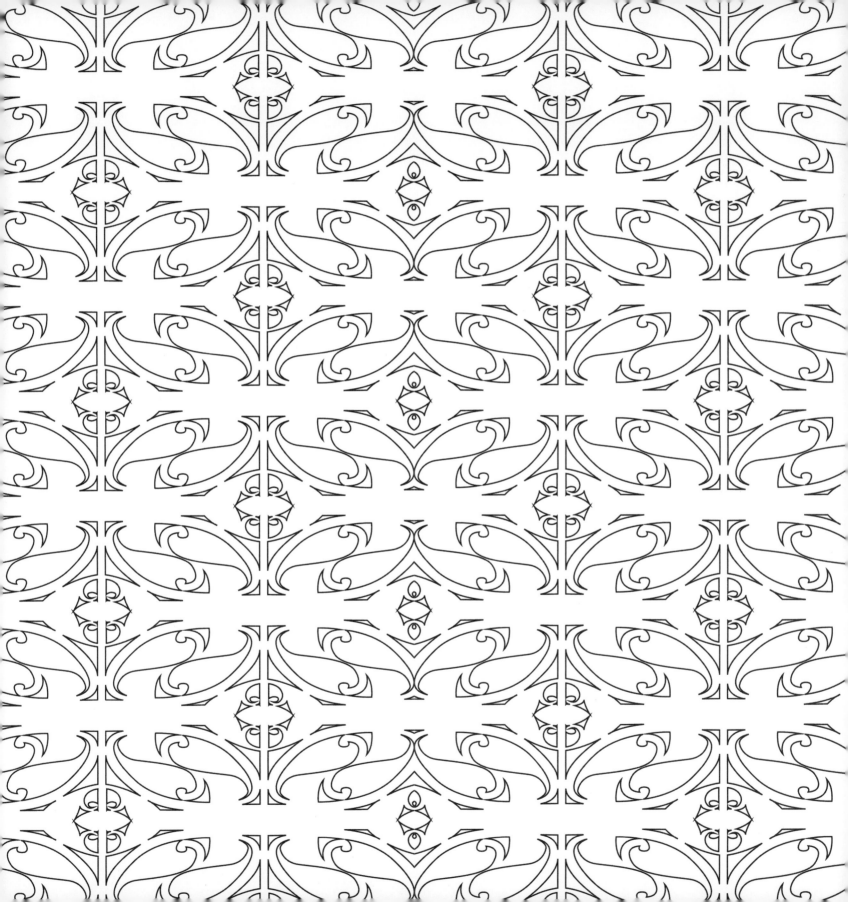

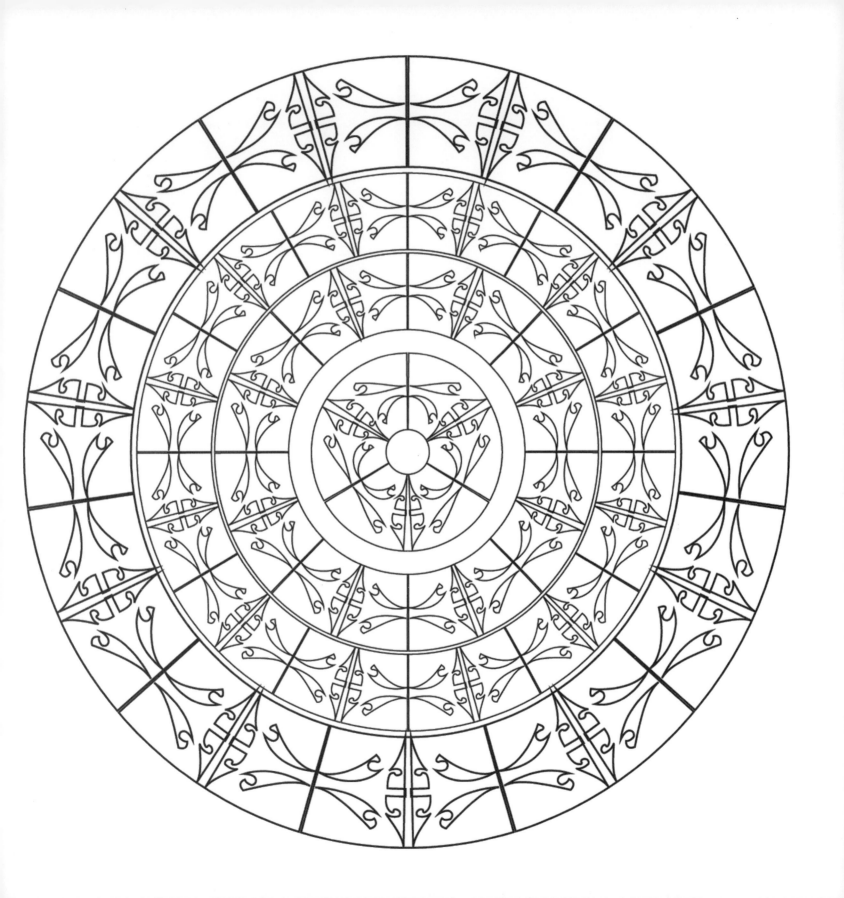

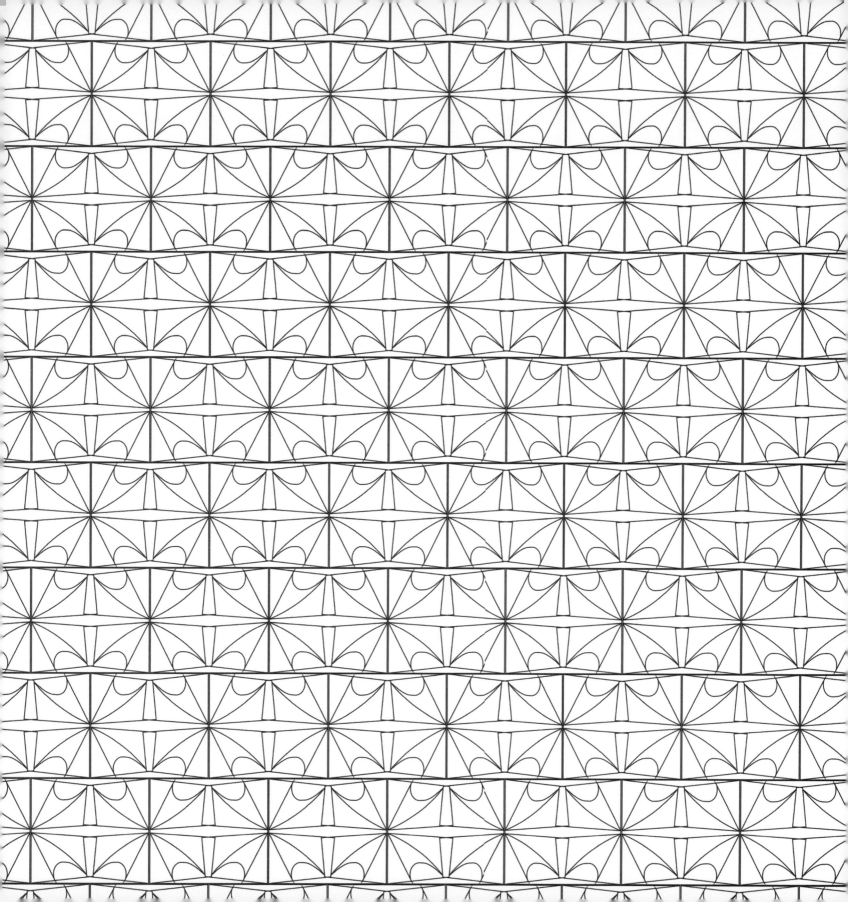

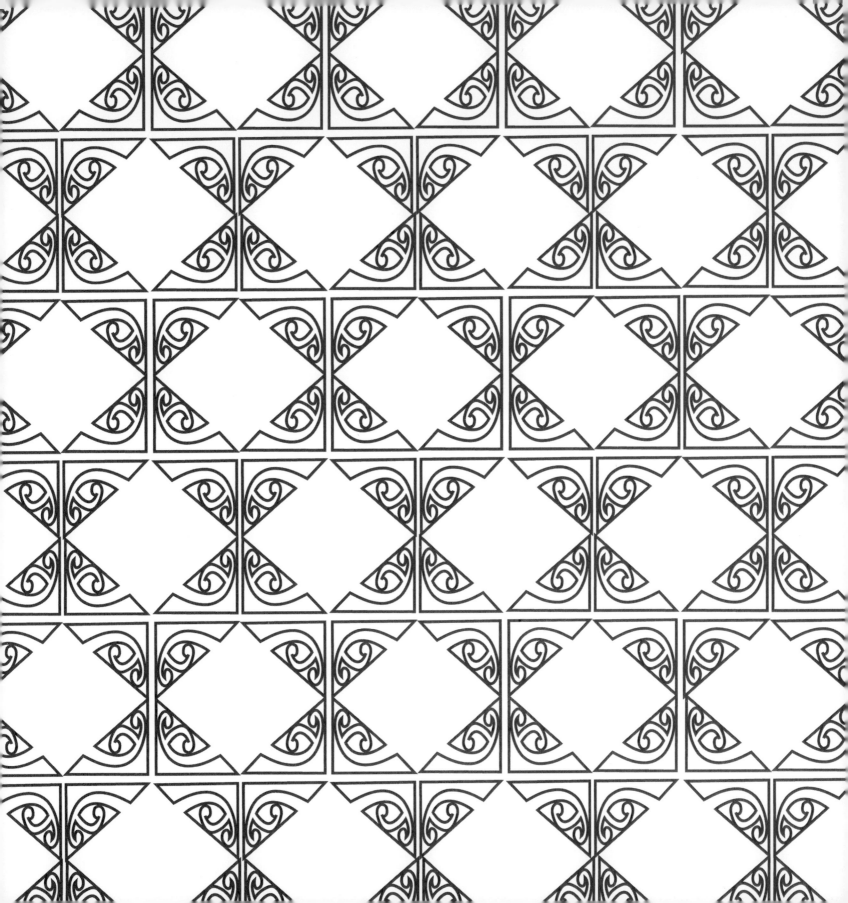

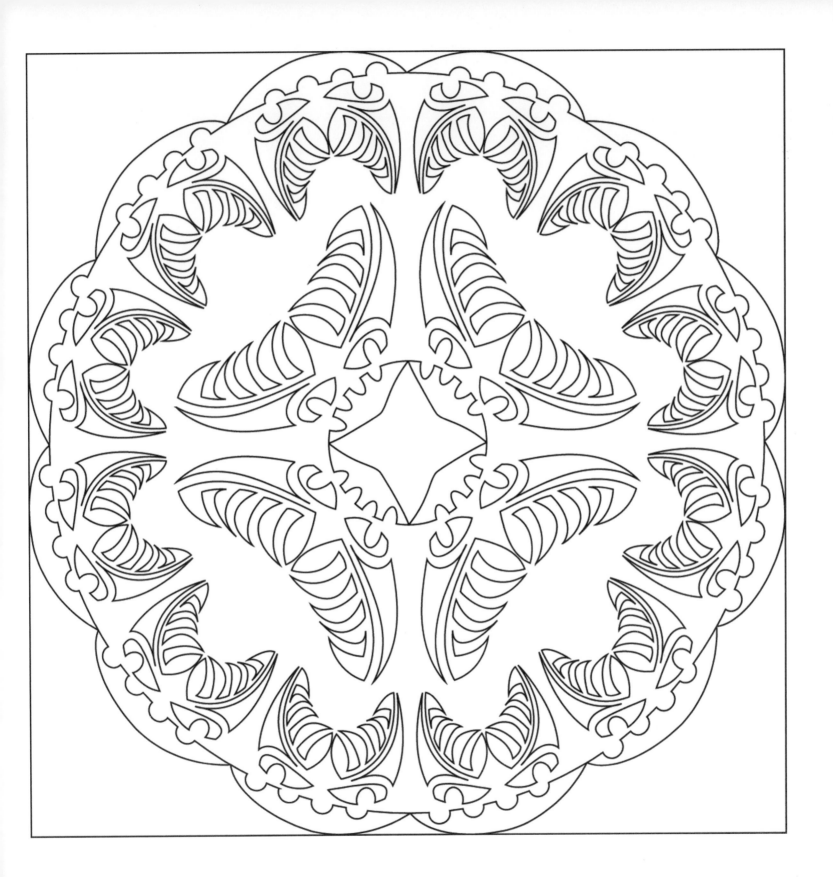

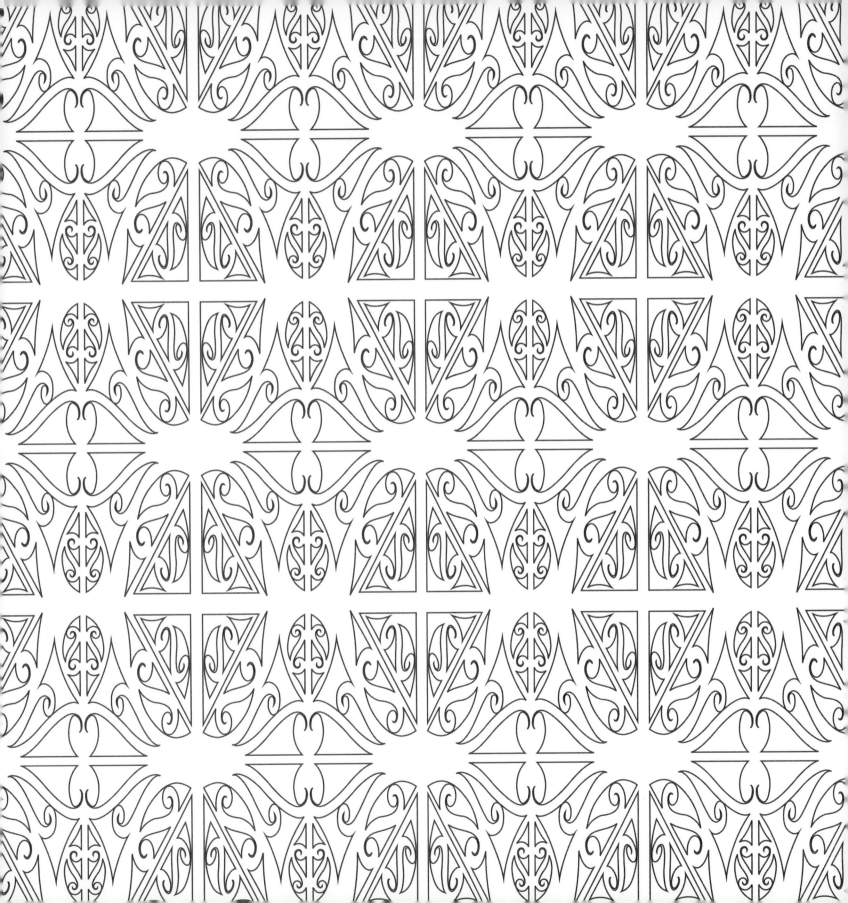

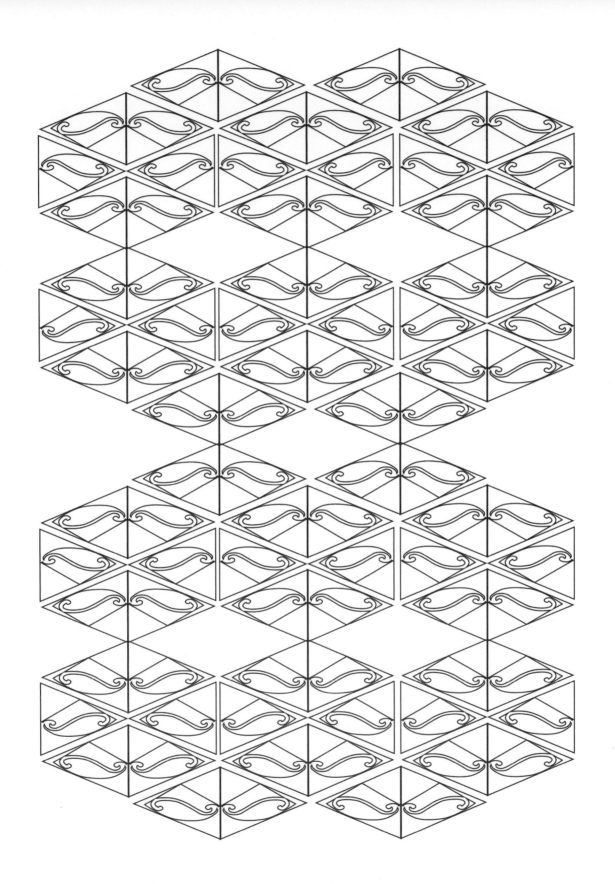

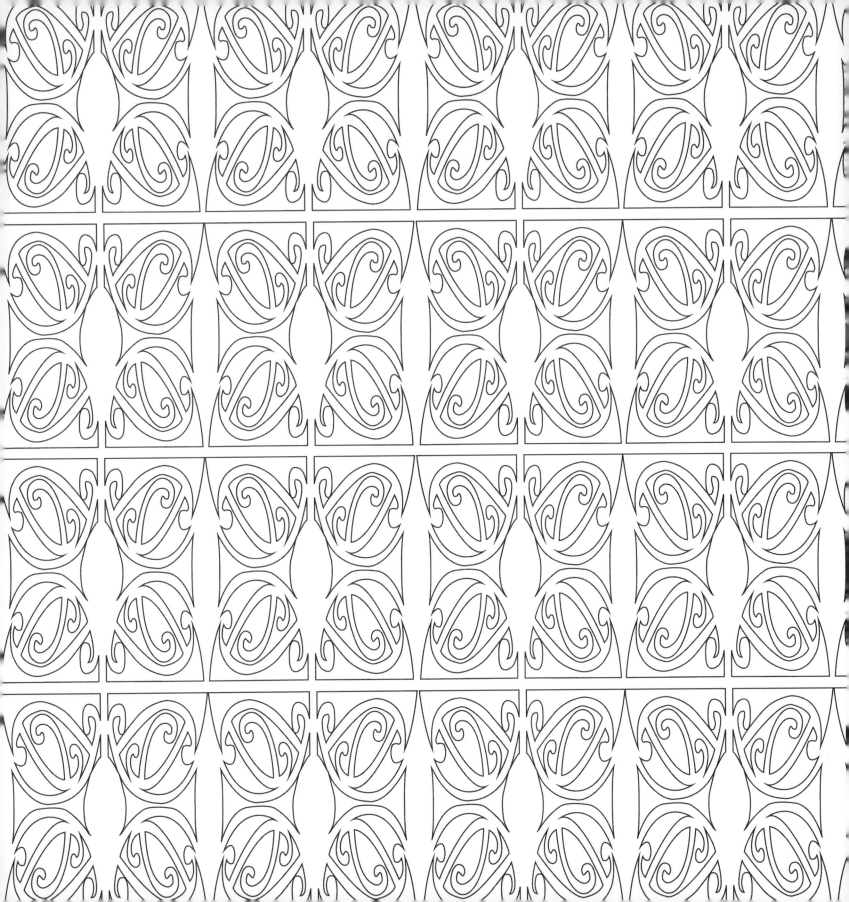

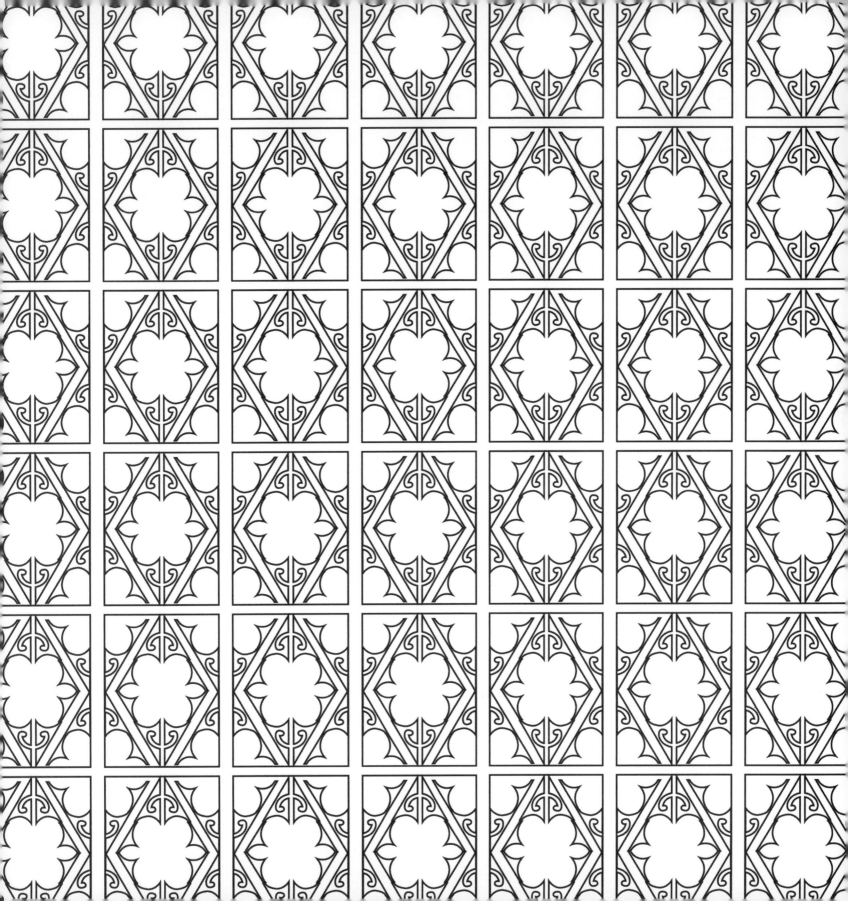

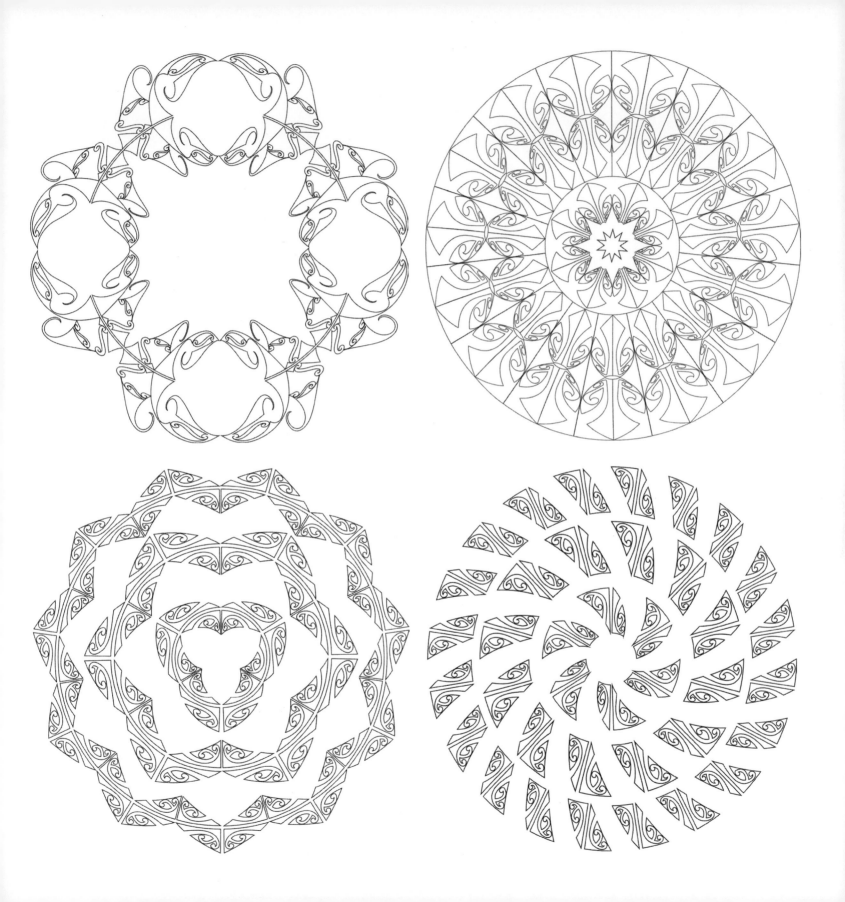

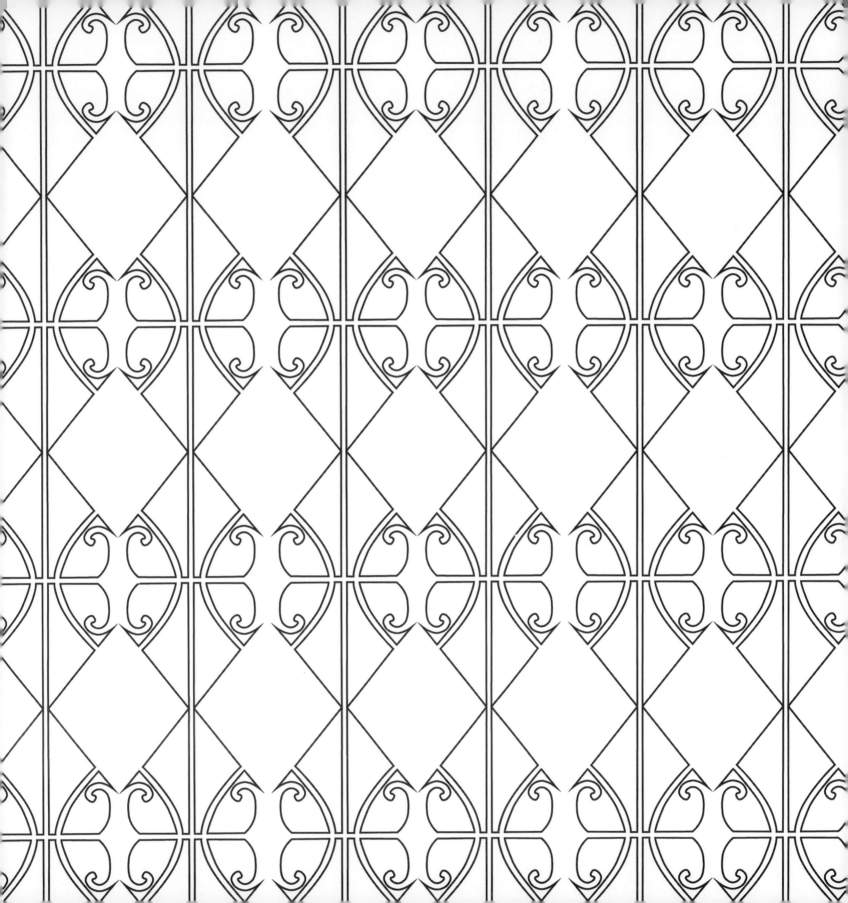

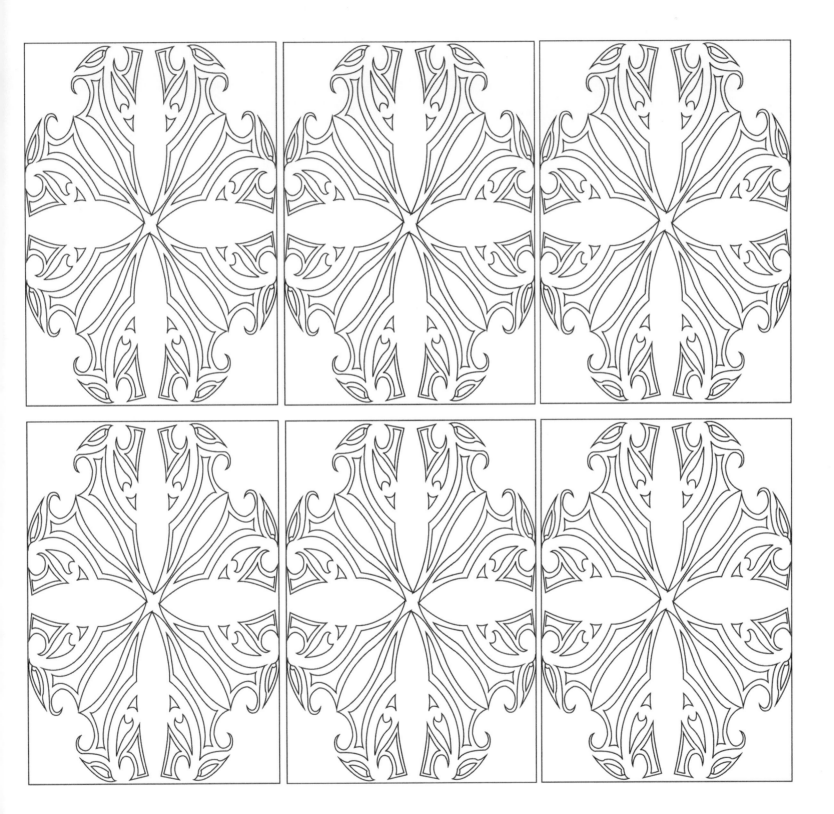

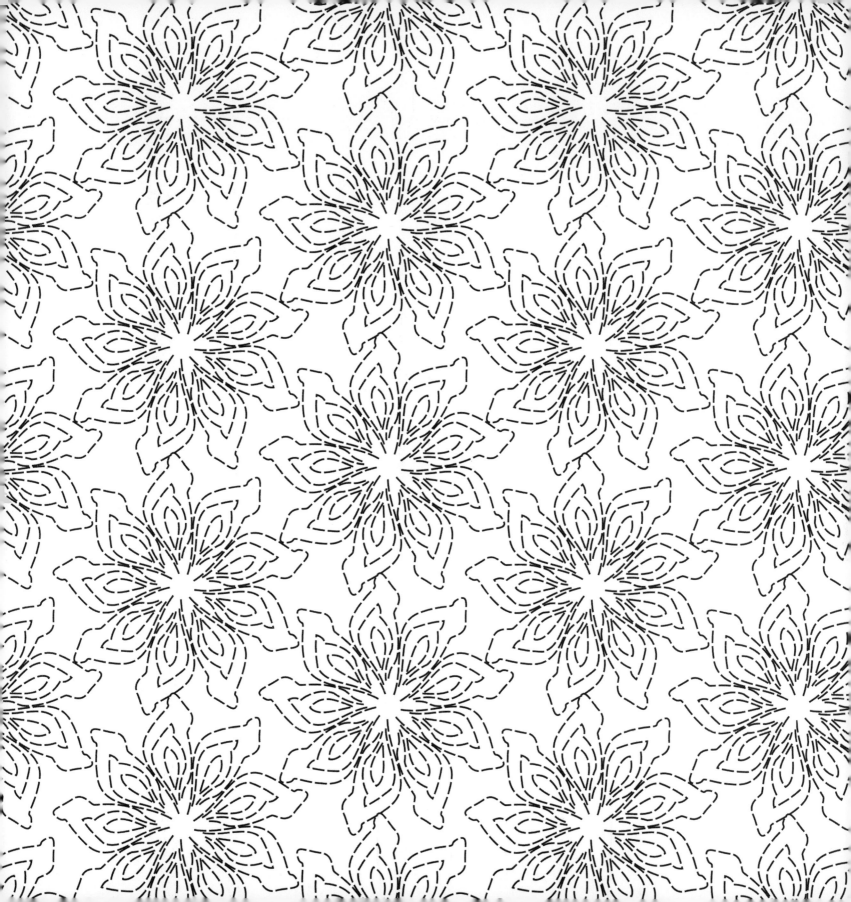

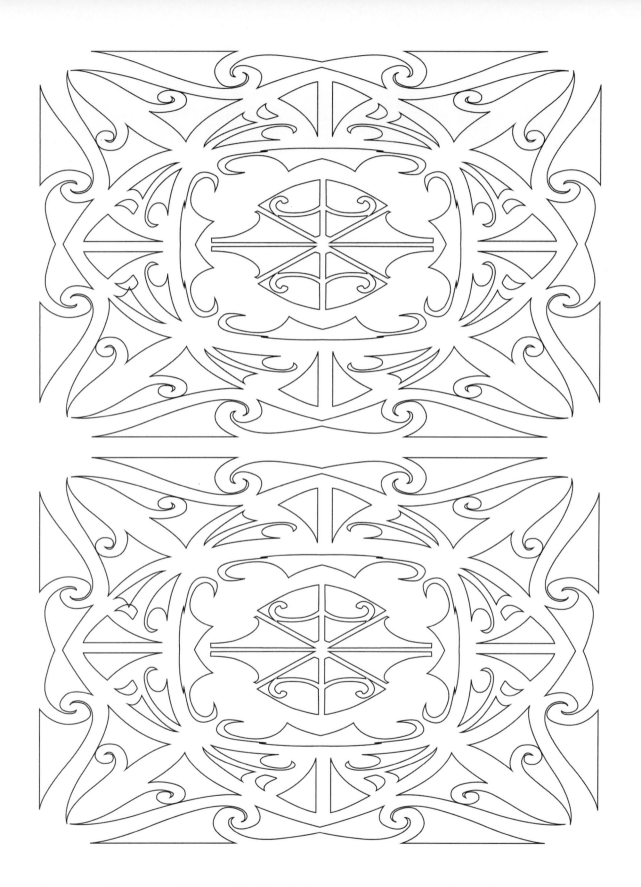

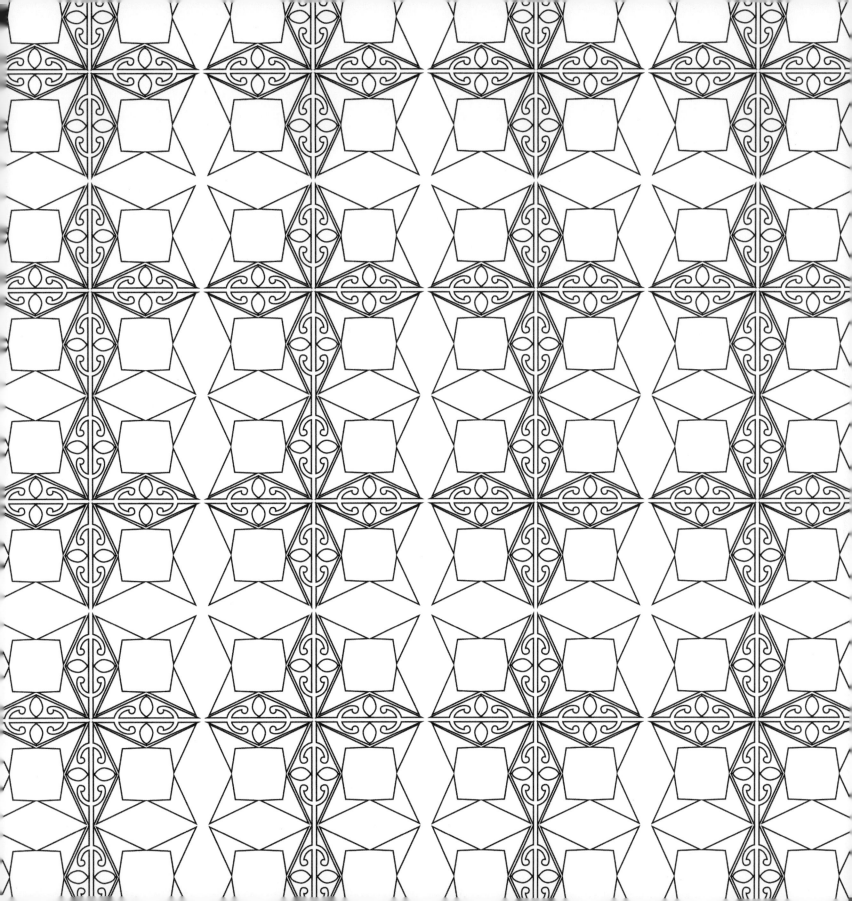

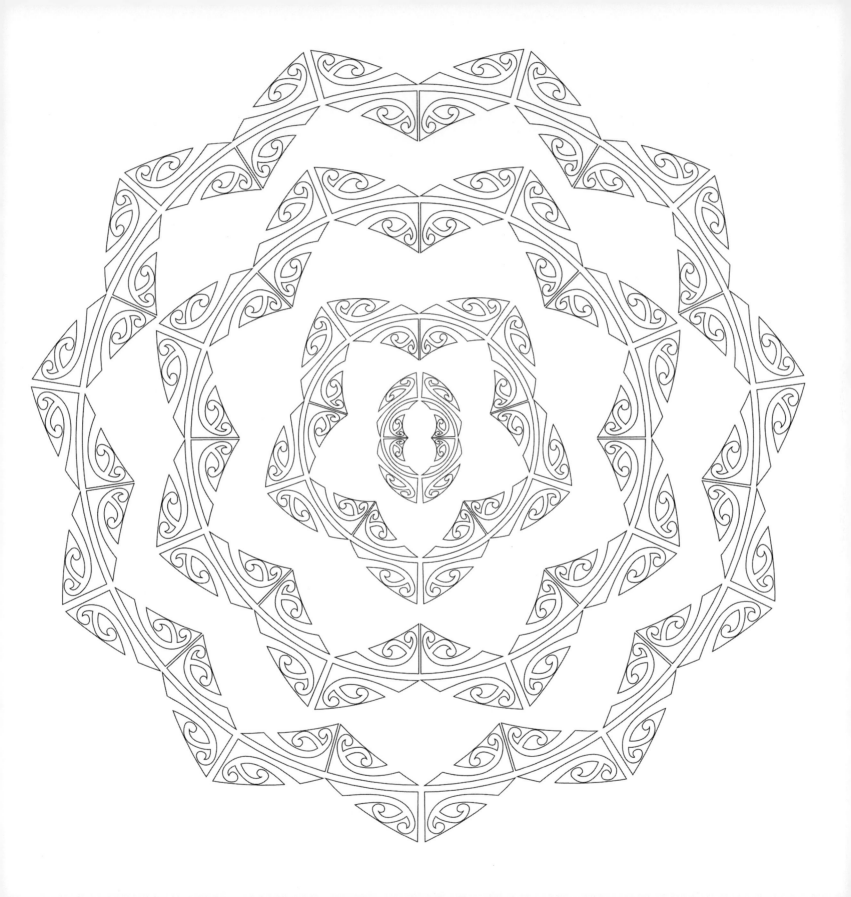

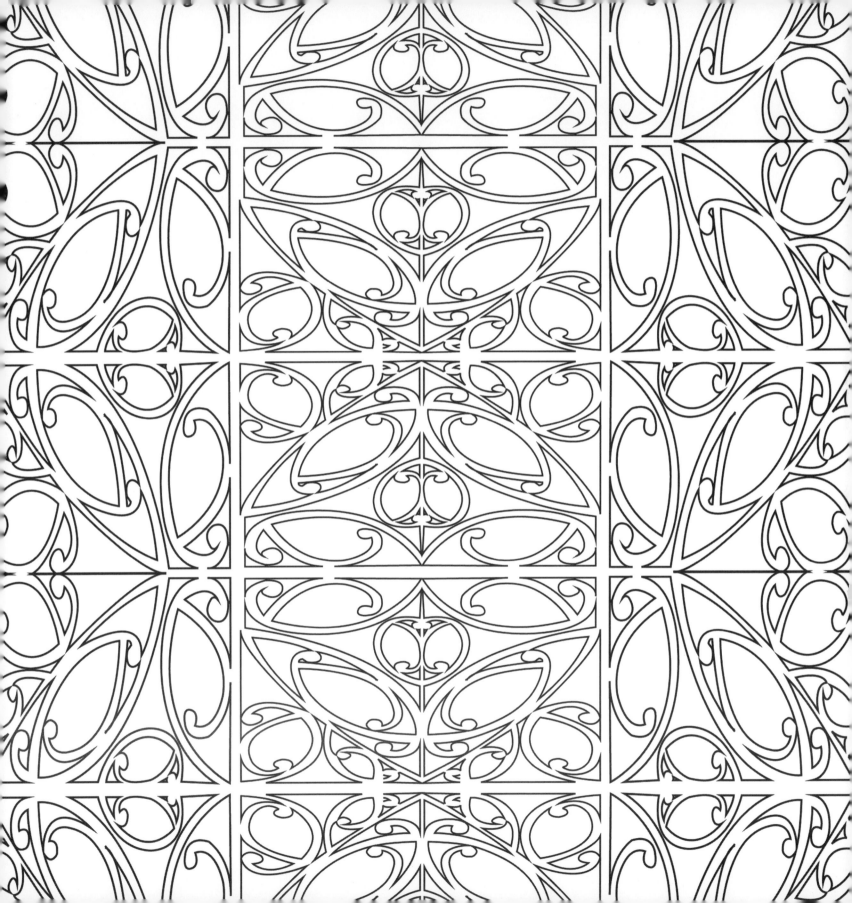

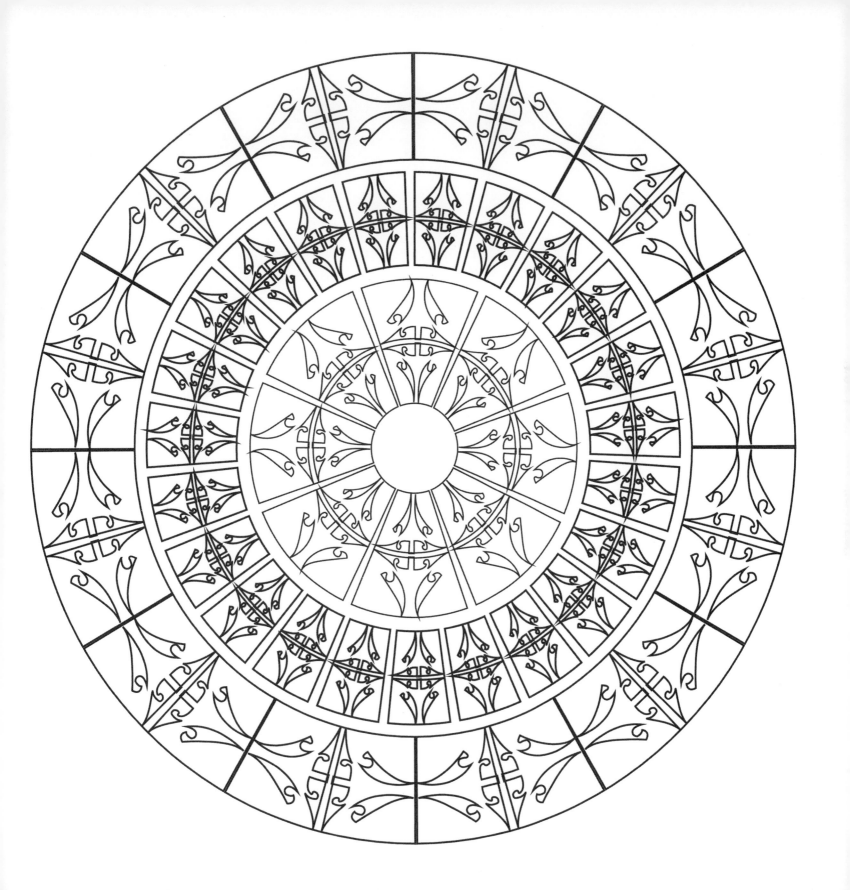

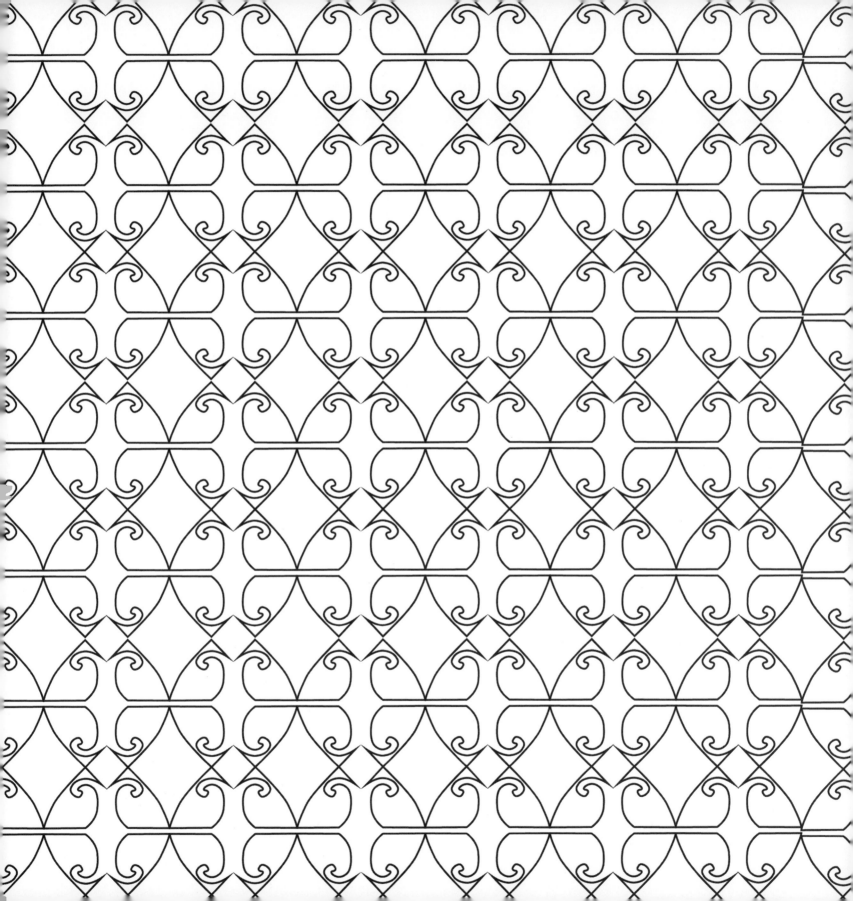

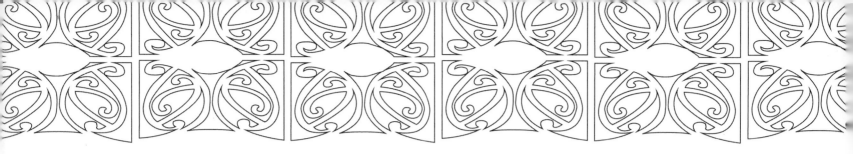

First published in 2015 by New Holland Publishers Pty Ltd
London • Sydney • Auckland

The Chandlery Unit 009 50 Westminster Bridge Road London SE1 7QY United Kingdom
1/66 Gibbes Street Chatswood NSW 2067 Australia
5/39 Woodside Avenue Northcote Auckland 0627 New Zealand

www.newhollandpublishers.com

A record of this book is held at the British Library, the National Library of Australia and NZ National Library.

ISBN 978 1 86966 432 9

Managing Director: Fiona Schultz
Designer: Lorena Susak
Production Director: Olga Dementiev
Printer: Toppan Leefung Printing Ltd

10 9 8 7 6 5 4 3

Keep up with New Holland Publishers on Facebook
www.facebook.com/NewHollandPublishers

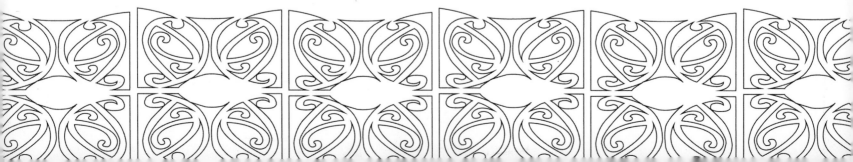